Devotions for the Golden Years

The Quiet Moment

by Jeanette Lockerbie

STANDARD PUBLISHING
Cincinnati, Ohio 3009

Library of Congress Cataloging in Publication Data

Lockerbie, Jeanette W.
The quiet moment.

1. Aged—Prayer-books and devotions—English.
I. Title.
BV4580.L63 1982 242'.65 82-7344
ISBN 0-87239-606-1

DEDICATION

In memory of my mother who taught me early to sing and love hymns; and my father who entered the kingdom at age 68 and quietly served his Savior for a quarter of a century.

Contents

The Springtime of Faith

Genesis 8:18-22

I am a lover of sweet peas. Their delicate pastels and sweet fragrance do something good for me. One spring day a friend, whose fine blossoms I had openly admired, handed me a tiny packet. "It's your sweet-pea seeds," she explained with a smile that added even more to the promise of flowers to come.

Earlier we had discussed the planting procedure, so that very day I followed the directions and planted my seeds. As I did I thought, "This takes some faith! I've seen pebbles on the beach that appeared to have more life in them than these tiny, wizened-up seeds." But, because I had faith in what I could not see, I watered the seeds and left them in God's good earth, in His care.

I did one other thing that day. I circled the date on my calendar and noted, "Today I planted sweet-pea seeds." What I was actually expressing in that note to myself was, "I'm expecting something definite to happen as a result of my seed planting—and I'll be counting the days."

God's promises can be likened to seed, and putting our faith to work is a form of seed planting. In an act as specific as planting a seed in the ground, we can figuratively hide a promise in our heart and expect something definite to result. And there is nothing faithless about recording the date on which we demonstrated our faith in this way.

We may never see the process by which God honors our faith, any more than we can observe nature at work in bringing to fruition the "dead" seed we plant in faith. Unknown to us, God works out the miracle(s) which produces the beautiful answer to the beautiful needs we have expressed in prayer. Just as we refrain from digging up a seed to see if it is growing, so we exercise patience when we await God's response to our faith planting. Meanwhile, we keep the soil of our soul well-watered through the Word and believing prayer.

When the enemy of our souls would come with his attempt to demoralize us, to break down our trust in God with his diabolical "I *told* you it wouldn't grow," let's meet his onslaughts as others before us have done. The indomitable Dr. Roland Bingham clung to God's promises with,

> Faith, mighty faith, the promises sees
> And looks to God alone;
> Laughs at impossibilities
> And cries, "It shall be done."

To think about and do:

It's my responsibility to plant the faith seed.

It's God's good pleasure to honor my faith.

The Most Comforting Words Ever Spoken

Genesis 28:10-15

In a small-group Bible study, someone raised the question, "What's the most comforting verse in the Bible?"

Immediately each one responded with a different verse. This is understandable; we all reach into God's Word for what will meet our present greatest need. So each one in the group gave the "right" answer.

There is, however, one verse—even a part of the verse—which is all-encompassing as a need meeter. Just five words: *"I will never leave you."*

Let's look at it a word at a time.

I—Who is the *I* who makes such a powerful promise? For any promise is just as solid, just as reliable, as the one who makes it. Is the person able to keep the promise no matter what? Or are there "ifs" in the fine print?

Will—This denotes determination. What makes the person feel so confident he can follow through? Is he possibly a person with a degree of arrogance? Does he really mean, "I *will,*" or is he just saying words?

Never—Now here's a strong word! A word to be used with caution by sensible people. To be sure, we throw it around, "I'll never do this or that again." ("Never" is akin to "always"; another extravagant promise we rarely make good on.) When we humans make "never" promises, then because we cannot control all the circumstances, we fail the one to whom we've made the promise, we create the cynical reaction, "Promises, promises!"

Leave—This is one of the most poignant words in the English language. We hate to see a loved one leave. I well remember a sad faced Cambodian young woman whom I interviewed saying, "Our king left us." In that king were bound up all his people's hopes for personal and national survival. Our King will never leave us.

You—This makes it personal. God said it to Jacob. The writer to the Hebrews reiterated it for all of us: you and me (Hebrews 13:5).

Put it all together and we have God's inviolate assurance to us that He will be with us, wherever we are and whatever our circumstances. Here are five words to sink our teeth into as we face each day. And, as if that were not enough, the verse goes on "nor forsake" you.

To think about and do:

Has God ever *not* kept His promise to me? Never—so today I will not doubt.

When You Feel That God Has Forgotten You

Exodus 3:1-8

Do you feel sometimes that you're off in a lonely desert, or some backwater that everybody's forgotten? Have you ever come to the place that you think even God doesn't know where you are—worse, that He doesn't *care?*

Even God's people have such feelings at times. So we can empathize with Moses in his desert experience. How often must he have looked back to the days when he was *somebody* in the Egyptian court. We can imagine his gloomy thoughts: *sheep and more sheep—and nothing better to look forward to.*

But one day everything changed! After that Moses never knew a routine day for the rest of his life, for God came to him with a challenge. First, however, the Lord dispelled any idea that He had forgotten His people. God said,

"I have surely *seen* . . .
"I have *heard* . . .
"I *know* . . .
"I am *come down* to deliver them"

God has not changed since that episode.

He knows where you are. He knows your thoughts, your longings, your discouragements, your hopes, and your fears.

God has His unique ways of speaking to us (there was only one burning bush). One day—it can be *today*—out of the seeming "nothing" kind of job you're doing—at home or anywhere else—God will break through the monotony. He will speak to you as only He can. He speaks most often through His Word—suddenly a word or a verse will leap off the page and be *just for you.* Or, God may use someone else to convey His message; but you will recognize it as from God to meet your special need.

In my own life I've come to look for and expect good surprises from God: "serendipities" some folk call them.

God uses people who are already busy; not those who are sitting around bemoaning their fate. So it pays to be doing something, and there are no lack of things to do for Him. As for feeling we have no future, listen to this:

> "I know the plans I have for you, says the Lord. They are for good and not for evil, to give you a future and a hope" (Jeremiah 29:11).

To think about and do:

I'll do something worthwhile today—and who knows what God has in store for me!

What—
Love Myself!

Leviticus 19:18; Mark 12:28-31

Most of us grew up with the Ten Commandments, and that's good. But we cannot discount the fact that Jesus gave us *two* and declared, "There is none other commandment greater than these."

Love the Lord our God
Love our neighbor as ourself

That shouldn't be too hard: two commandments rather than ten. But Jesus also said that He didn't come to nullify the Commandments. So there must be more to it.

Loving God is four-dimensional; it isn't a vague purely emotional love. It's premised on the great doctrinal, *"Hear, O Israel; The Lord our God is one Lord."*

He is to have first place in our *heart.*

He is to have first place in our *soul*—the worship and adoration part of us—the *spiritual* realm.

In our *mind*—the meditating, thinking, decision-making area—we are to put God first.

We are to love Him with all our *strength:* the doing, the practical expression of love. The thing that can make a difference in the world around us.

But that's not the end of it—all encompassing as it may seem.

Now we come to the part about loving our neighbor as ourself. Nothing difficult about the first part. It's easy to love my neighbor in a general "Good morning, how are you today?" way. But loving as I love myself! I have to think about that.

Christian teaching says, *"Don't* love yourself. That's haughtiness and pride." So, if my love for my neighbor is dependent on *my love for me,* poor neighbor!

How did Jesus mean for us to love ourselves? On what basis?

Is it not that we are God's workmanship, and that in His sight we are worthwhile beings—we are not worms of the dust. Many things in the Bible assure us that God loves us, God created us, and then He redeemed us, ransomed us with the highest ransom that was ever paid: the blood of Jesus. In ourselves we are not lovable, but God sees us through Christ. Really appropriating, *internalizing* this fact, will change our lives. We will have a healthy, balanced, Biblical self-image.

We *can* begin to learn to love ourselves. If we see other people through the same glasses with which we see ourselves, we'll begin to view our neighbors differently. We'll love them. We will have the same concern for them that we have for ourselves. We will be the kind of persons the Lord wants us to be.

To think about and do:

I can't be a good neighbor
until I love both myself and my neighbor.

Tomorrow's at My Door

Tomorrow's at my door—
  a young thing
  fresh and eager
  on tiptoe.

Tomorrow at my door
  what will you become
  as all too soon
  your hours wind down?

Just what I let you,
  you will be—
  so gladly I'll unlock the key
  and,
  welcome mat already
  spread,
  I'll bid you enter.

Grasshopper Mentality

Numbers 13:17-20, 27-33

Moses, at God's command, sent a fact-finding team, one man from each of the tribes of Israel, to research and report on what they found in Canaan. He gave them precise, practical things for which to look (vv. 18-20).

Their report read like, as we say today, "the good news and the bad news." They saw encouraging things in their forty-day search, including plenty of food.

The good news terminates abruptly with "Nevertheless," and they move onto the black side of the picture. They would have gone on and on in this vein, but Caleb silenced them with his, "Let's go. We are well able to take the land." But the majority of the twelve spies were against it. "They're *giants;* they'll *eat us up,"* they said. The concluding statement of this gloom-and-doom bunch was, "We were in our own sight as grasshoppers."

What causes such mentality? Among other things, failure to recognize who we are in God's sight. These were God's men, and ten of the twelve forgot it. (Joshua was on Caleb's side.) They failed to realize they were on God's business.

As Christians we all need to keep in mind who we are in the sight of God. He redeemed us at such a cost that we must be extremely valuable to Him (1 Peter 1:18).

We are His workmanship, created for something (Ephesians 2:10). We are not grasshoppers. We are not nothings. Some people say, "O Lord, make me nothing." God wants us to be something. Our prayers should reflect this attitude.

We are members of God's family (John 1:12) with all the rights and privileges of children.

These spies were right when they said, in effect, "They're too much for us." As long as we see ourselves as "grasshoppers," we will be defeated by circumstances and everything else. Their second comment was equally true: "So we were in their sight"—grasshoppers.

People judge us by what we project of ourselves. One of the soundest pieces of counsel I ever received was from my own son. I was moving into a totally new area—in every sense of the word—and I was apprehensive. At the airport, as my flight was called, he put his arm around me and said, "Mom, these people don't know you. Keep in mind that they will view you as they see how you view yourself."

Fortunately, as long as we are alive and breathing, we can change. We can move up from the grasshopper mentality to a healthy awareness of who and what we are, and go on to conquer life's giants. This is God's will for His highest creation.

To think about and do:

I am a child of God.

Today I'm going to feel and act like it.

Turn Another Page

1 Samuel 27:1-7

Listen to the conversation of people in a supermarket or on the street. So much of it is gloomy predictions or opinions:

"This inflation will kill me."

"Nobody cares one little bit about older folk."

"Our country was *never* in such bad shape." You can probably add ten more such dismal statements.

The fact that there may be some truth in the dreary talk adds no value. It just tends to depress the hearers, who are rarely in a position to do anything about the situation. Nevertheless, many of us fall into this bad-news trap.

David had fallen into this kind of trap concerning himself rather than conditions in general. He was predicting his own untimely death. Not only that, but he was talking of seeking refuge with the enemy, the Philistines! "Saul's going to kill me. I might as well go over to the enemy's side." David was discouraged and near despair.

How close that is to doubting God. In fact, the devil is a master at these three D's: discouragement, despair, and doubt.

Too bad David couldn't turn over a few pages

and read, as we can, "And the time that he reigned over Israel was forty years . . . And he died in a good old age, full of days, riches, and honor." (See 1 Chronicles 29: 26-28.)

David had certainly been used badly by King Saul. But he had proved God's power to save him—even from a giant!

Does your present set of circumstances seem too much for you to endure?

Do you dread the future?

Do you feel that perhaps God has forgotten you?

Does the way of the ungodly tempt you to forsake your faith?

Running away is never the answer. It wasn't for David; it isn't for you or me. There will be answers as you turn the pages; answers like:

"Commit thy way unto the Lord" (Psalm 37:5);

"I am with you alway" (Matthew 28:20);

"My peace I give unto you" (John 14:27);

"I will never leave thee, nor forsake thee" (Hebrews 13:5).

For your special, individual need, turn the pages and read until a verse leaps out at you as though it were written just for you.

Your days may be dark, but it is as true today as when Hudson Taylor said it, "The future is as bright as the promises of God."

To think about and do:

I can let my mind dwell on gloomy probabilites,

Or I can turn from them and focus on God's faithfulness.

A Crisis or an Opportunity?

Psalm 11:1-7

We would be blind optimists if we were not aware of these critical days in which we live—when the very things that made our nation great are under attack. The Chinese have no single word for "crisis"; rather it's an expression that has the dual meaning of "danger" and "opportunity." Worth thinking about, isn't it?

Yes, conditions are frightening—but there are opportunities. The question comes to us as it did to David, "What shall we do?"

This question reveals a healthy attitude toward the situation. But, in the face of grim facts, we have to ask, "What should I *not* do?" For example, it will help if we do not:

Wring our hands, or throw up our hands, giving the impression that we have nowhere to turn; that God is dead.

Give up in heart and spirit, demonstrating that we have lost faith in the God who has seen us through until now.

Join the pessimists who demoralize even the Christians around them.

None of these can help one little bit.

David is a good model for what we should do. We need to fix our mind on what is *not crumbling.* We need to reassure ourselves that the foundation of God stands sure . . . the Lord knows those that are His. (See 2 Timothy 2:19.)

God has not moved. He has not gone off on a vacation. He has not turned over the reins of government. If we understand this, we can have a soundly based sense of security. This gives us an opportunity rather than a crisis.

People around us need to know what we know: that the seat of power and ultimate authority is not in Washington, not in London, not even in Jerusalem. It is where it has always been—with God. Well might we say, and believe and take comfort in,

> God is still on His throne,
> And He will remember His own.

This doesn't mean that we will escape all trials and trauma. While we can rejoice and feel secure, Psalm 11 also reminds us that God is weighing *us* in His balances. Sometimes He has to send the refining fire upon us. We will never have to account for the doings and destruction of a godless, humanistic, secular society. But God sees us too—and sees through us—and we will have to account for ourselves.

To think about and do:

Today, because I am His, I have the opportunity to help a neighbor see hope beyond the crisis.

You Don't Have to Become a Statistic

Psalm 31:13-19

Without the balance of God's Word, it would be difficult to maintain a good outlook. Around the clock we're bombarded with bad news and dire prophecies by the media. The mails add their contribution with brochures and pamphlets telling of recent findings of how many people in this country will die of this or that disease; of how many hospital beds are occupied by mental patients (and the slim chance we have of escaping that fate). Hourly we hear grim crime statistics, reeled off as though it's inevitable that we will all fall victim.

It's enough to cause us to worry. But worry is no answer. As a radio pastor tells his listeners, "Worry is the interest we pay on something before it happens."

It may never *happen!* There's a fifty percent chance that it won't.

Fortunately for our sanity, Christians have a proven deterrant to gloomy fears and depression. We have the promises of God. He has not promised that we will have no trials or problems, that we will go through life unscarred. Life is not like that.

God has promised something infinitely richer for His people. He did not say, "I will keep you *out of trouble.*" He said, "I will be with you in trouble; I will deliver you."

> When thou passest through the waters,
> Deep the waves may be, and cold;
> But Jehovah is thy refuge
> And His promise is thy hold.
> He, the living Lord, has said it,
> And I know His word is true;
> When thou passest through the waters,
> Thou shalt not go down—but *through*.

The Bible tells us that the Lord is a *present help* (Psalm 46:1). We do not receive grace and strength to bear the trial *until it is upon us*. Corrie Ten Boom has talked and written about this beautiful truth. When did her father give her the train ticket? Not until the train arrived in the station. She didn't need it till then, and her father knew that. So Corrie learned not to worry.

Faith will keep us from worry. If we have faith, we know that God *will* be there with us meeting whatever our need *when the time comes*.

To think about and do:

Why should I fret over "the bad news"?

The "good news" is that *my times are in God's hand.*

What I Can Do

What can "just me" do?
I'll plant some seeds of love—today—
For the tomorrow at my door.
And grow it will, for, God,
A part of Your own heart is in each seed
Since You are living love.

But, Lord, that mine be more
Than loving warmth 'tween You and me,
Teach me what You would have me *do*
In love *today*
For someone who from care and more
Can't face tomorrow at the door.

I cannot plant these seeds
Except You plant them first in me.
My heart's Your soil,
Lord plant Christ's love in me
And may I tenfold—that and *more*—
Invest in the tomorrow at my door.

Help! I'm Lost

Psalm 32:7-11; 48:14

Some people instinctively know their way around. Even in new surroundings they have no difficulty in locating places they're looking for. Then there are the rest of us. We are sort of wandering souls who don't have this built-in radar, and for whom getting lost is a lifelong frustration.

It's no fun feeling lost. I recall a rainy, cold Saturday evening when I set out to attend a party honoring a friend who had just received her doctorate. In spite of the little map imprinted on the invitation, I got hopelessly lost. At one cross section, in sheer frustration—and feeling a bit scared—I just *cried.* Then I said, "Lord, I don't know how to get where I'm supposed to go; and now *I don't know my way home!*" Through the help of others, the Lord guided me on my way and home.

Humiliating as it can be sometimes, I praise the Lord for lessons He keeps teaching me as I have to lean on Him. Doing all I can for myself, I trust the Lord to guide me however He will.

"I will guide you" is God's promise. Some people give verbal directions; others offer a map. (I can't read maps.) God says, in effect, "I know the way. I've been there. Let me show you." And who wouldn't rather have a guide than a map!

There is nothing temporary about God's guidance. He doesn't take us to a certain corner of life and say, "There, you'll make it all right on your own now." Psalm 48:14 assures us,

> *"For this God is our God for ever and ever: he will be our guide even unto death."*

What about the spiritual ramifications of knowing we are lost? What difference does that make? All the difference in time and eternity. Until we realize we are lost, we will not be fit candidates for salvation. Luke 19:10 tells us:

> *"For the Son of man is come to seek and to save that which was lost."*

So there are benefits for the person who knows he is lost and is willing to admit it—and seeks help.

There are people—sometimes very close friends even—who can't understand this problem because they have never been plagued by it. They may construe it as affectation on our part or a bid for attention. But God understands.

To think about and do:

I don't have to worry about finding the way to Heaven;

I just have to follow Him who *is* the Way.

One Day at a Time

Psalm 37:1-5

The Scripture for the neighborhood women's Bible study was Psalm 37. A member who was well up in years when she became a believer, always had questions, for the Bible was still a new book to her.

"Will someone please tell me," she asked, "how I can commit my way to the Lord? It seems so vague—so—oh, I don't know how to explain it," she fumbled. "I just don't know what it's *saying.*"

After some thought, one of the members offered to share what the verse said to her.

"I used to feel the way you've just expressed and for the same reason," she explained. "Then the Lord led me to see how I could make it simple. Just change 'way' to '*d*ay'—one letter different. Instead of trying to commit my way, I translated it to committing each day. I can *handle* that."

A wise suggestion? I think we can conclude that it is, since our "way" in the context of verse 5 is the *sum of our days.* As Annie Johnson Flint has written,

One day at a time,
And the day is His day;
He hath numbered its hours,
Though they haste or delay.

A related question might be, "What does commit mean, in the practical sense?" Sometimes contrasts are good for clarifying: Take the two words commit and consign. We commit some things; we consign others. For example, we consign trash to the garbage can. We just want to be rid of it. On the other hand, something we value we commit into safe keeping. We commit (trust) important documents to a safety deposit box.

The apostle Paul had this straight when he wrote:

"I know whom I have believed, and am
persuaded that he is able to keep
that which I have committed"
(2 Timothy 1:12).

What had Paul committed? His *eternal destiny*. It is the all-time most critical commitment we will ever make. The assurance of our eternal life can be safely committed to Christ alone: "Christ in you, the hope of glory."

Persuaded, as Paul was, that Christ is able to keep, should we not commit each day as it comes to Him?

To think about and do:

I do the committing; God takes over—
and I've nothing to lose

What's Wrong With Being a Do-Gooder?

Psalm 37:3-6

When you hear someone say, "He/she is a do-gooder," what image comes to your mind? All too often the term has a negative connotation.

Does this need to be so? Can't "do good" mean just what it says?

Recently I was impressed with this idea as I was reading this Psalm 37. The words "Trust in the Lord, and do good" captured my attention. I just stopped there and considered what I was reading.

God himself gives us two brief directives:

1. Trust Him
2. Do good

The rewards for doing both are clearly spelled out.

Most of us, I assume, would strongly assert that as believers we trust the Lord. Honesty, however, might make us admit to less certainty about how much good we do in the world. Yet both injunctions are from God. Both are possible or the Lord would not explicitly ask it of us.

Trusting God is a state of heart and mind.

Doing good can be called a state of hands and feet, a spirit of willingness to help other people. Together, better than anything else, they can demonstrate to a cynical neighbor that Christianity is credible.

"What specific good can I do?" you may be asking. That will depend on the kind of person you are, on the needs around you, and on your ability and willingness to reach out and do something to help.

Some people have the gift of mercy—the gift of helping. These are natural do-gooders. For others, and I may be one of them, doing good is not the first thing that comes to mind. Even so, we are all accountable to God for how we obey His directives.

There is rarely a time when we can't find a way to do a kindness, to reach out in love and compassion. It may be by telephone, by writing a note to a lonely individual, or by giving up some pet project to be a good neighbor and friend for a little while.

Doing good involves time. There's no way we can give of ourselves without surrendering some of our precious time. We say of some people, "Where do they find the time?" That's no mystery. We all have the same allotment of time: twenty-four hours to the day. And one of God's intentions is that we use part of it in doing good.

To think about and do:

Jesus "went about doing good."

As His follower I want to do something good for somone today.

The Plus of Good Expectations

Psalm 62:1-5

How important are our expectations?

They can be all-important, for they are determiners of how optimistic or pessimistic we become. They can influence our whole outlook.

I know a man, a top executive, who is an habitual early riser. When a colleague commented on this trait, he grinned and answered, with a twinkle in his eyes, "I *have* to, I just can't wait to see what God is up to in the morning."

This attitude of expectancy keeps him looking for the good things. He is one of those who regards each day as the great possibility. Such optimism is contagious, just as is its opposite.

Happy expectations do not guarantee freedom from problems, but they do keep us from suffering "before the fact." Thus they help us to better cope with what life sends our way.

The person who can see only the gloomy side ahead needs our understanding. He or she may have grown up without ever having a pair of rose-colored glasses. Maybe they had bad experiences: their good expectations were crushed by other people until they became cynics and gloom peddlers. (Unless they will let us help them, it's healthier for us to shy away from them.)

As Christians, whose expectations are from *God,* we need never become disillusioned. Like David, I can determine not to be greatly moved. I will *not* expect the worst in any situation.

Our expectations are closely tied into both our *faith* and our *hope.* In a sense it's true that according to our expectations it will be unto us.

Sadly, Christians are not exempt from this negative attitude that's all too prevalent. And the "Why should I expect anything good to come *my* way?" complex extends to "Why should *I* expect that God will answer my prayer?" Faithlessness then turns into hopelessness.

Fortunately, as long as we are alive and breathing, we *can change.* It's a process, not an instant transformation. So the sooner we recognize the need to change and ask God to forgive us and help us, the happier we will be.

The new attitude of positive expectations keeps us in a spirit of happy excitement about today and tomorrow. We might even come to the place where *we* can hardly wait to get up in the morning to see what God is up to!

One thing we can be sure of is that His mercies are new every morning.

To think about and do:

Good expectations? Poor expectations?
The choice is mine.

I'll Show Appreciation

God, did You whisper appreciation
is the seed too long unlovingly I've hoarded,
failing You and Your Creation?
I hear You, God.
I'll do it.
I'll show and say
Today—*today*.
I appreciate you and you and you.
Not what you do,
Not what you have to give,
Not where you live—but *you*.
I appreciate you.
This seed I'll plant today.
This I can do today
For the tomorrow at my door.

It May Depend on You

Psalm 78:1-8

Who is making God real to today's children? You may feel a desire to be the one to lead a child in this direction.

"But," you rationalize, "children are such sophisticated little people. They have so much, and they seem to know so much."

True. Most of their toys are far beyond our understanding. Nevertheless, I've never known a little boy or girl who didn't like stories. Not long ago I listened in on a conversation between two adorable four-year-olds. They were trying one-upmanship on each other. "My grandma buys me the nicest toys, and candy, too," bragged Susie.

"Oh, but *my* grandma tells me stories and she *reads to me,*" Lory countered. Her tone held a you-can-keep-your-old-toys note.

So what were they expressing? The one was saying that her grandmother spent *money* on her; the other was speaking of a grandmother who spent *time* with her.

It does take time to sit down and read or tell a story (and one is never enough, as anyone who does it will agree). But how rewarding the result can be!

We don't all have "Little House on the Prairie" tales to recount, but we do have our own individual experiences to relate. And we have the wonderful stories in the Bible.

Some years ago I visited a young relative who was sick, and he asked me to read him a story. There was a Bible in his room. I reached for it and read the story of the boy Samuel. Well, about a week later, his mother phoned and asked, "Will you please tell me where I can find the story about God talking to a little boy, by name?" She sounded exasperated. "I can't find it, and Jon's bugging me to read it to him."

We never know which Bible truth a child's mind will latch on to. We never know the effect it will have on him for life.

We can feed into a child our own assurance—*from experience*—of a God who delights to answer prayer. By not hiding from children these things that praise and honor God (v. 4), we may start a chain reaction that can result in future generations knowing and making them known to their children.

Somebody has to ignite the spark. What a privilege to be that one!

To think about and do:

Somebody cared enough to tell me the sweetest story ever told.

Today I can start passing it on.

The Gracious Giving God

Psalm 84:8-12

Sometimes God is portrayed as a heavenly tyrant sitting up there and looking down on us saying, "Now what can I deprive them of today?" But everything we know of Him from the Bible and our own experience tells us God is not like that. He is the greatest of all givers as John 3:16 affirms over and over.

Then why is my prayer not answered? We often question and pout. Has not God said He wouldn't withhold any good thing from us? Yes. It's worth noting that in the same verse He is called our sun and shield: the sun for warmth, light, and promotion of growth; the shield for protection (sometimes from ourselves and our prayer requests).

God is in the giving, not the withholding, business. But He has laid down conditions: (1) It has to be a *good* thing we are asking for. But what is 'good'? How can we know that what we want the Lord to give us or do for us is good? We can't trust our own heart to tell us, for the heart is deceitful as Jeremiah tells us (17:9).

I am no theologian, but I can pass on something the Lord is teaching me along this line. Like you, I've done my own share of praying—maybe *demanding* would be more accurate at times—for something I've desperately wanted and which seemed to me a good thing.

2. *Upright* is the second requirement for answered prayer. David gives us his secret: "Cleanse thou me from secret faults . . . then shall I be upright" (Psalm 19:13). It is as we pray this prayer that the Holy Spirit—like the sunshine—sheds light on hidden areas of *un*-uprightness. Then as we seek with God's help to overcome these sins, to correct our less than Christian behavior, we grow in grace and in discernment as to what is "good." We grow in what can help to keep us upright so God can grant us the desires of our heart. And in the process we become better persons.

In dealing with our own children, we've exercised responsibility in heeding their every "gimme." Why? Because we knew more than they did. We loved them enough to protect them, often against their wishes, from things we knew were not good.

Would we expect God to use less judgment? Would we want Him to? Does He love us less than we love our children?

As we look back through the years, we will probably admit thankfully that the Lord has graciously given, more times than He has in love *withheld,* the answer to our prayer.

To think about and do:

How much do I hinder my own prayers?

What do I need to change in order to be upright?

What You Have Going for You

Psalm 92:12-15

Over their teacups, Sara and her neighbor Anne were commiserating with each other. "What do we have left?" was the theme of their little pity party as they sat reinforcing each other's negative feelings. Finally Anne paused and said wistfully, "We must still be of some good in the world."

I suppose most of us have temporary spells of feeling we have outlived our usefulness, but it's much better to dwell on what we have because of God's goodness in allowing us to live a long life.

What are some of our most valuable assets?

Wisdom. Nobody is born wise, and some people do acquire more wisdom than others. Nevertheless, the mature years generally bring with them a fair measure of wisdom. This is something we can profitably share with those who are younger.

Experience. Just the fact of having lived long years has taught us many things. Of course, the cynic may gripe, "I haven't had sixty years' experience; I've had one year's experience *sixty times over!"*

Sound Judgment. No one will question that a grandparent will normally make a more sensible decision than his grandchild. This ability to be discerning in decision making is the product of both wisdom and experience. We live and learn and generally profit by our mistakes. As Dr. Ralph Byron, noted Christian surgeon, once remarked to me, "Good judgment is developed through poor judgment." Obviously this is so by reason of the fact that we have to live with the consequences of our decisions.

Tolerance. Little things do not trouble us as they once did. We have more patience with the foibles of others, and with the trials life sends our way. We are less easily provoked.

Increased Faith. Life with Christ has been (and still is) a process of trusting Him and finding Him always faithful. We can stand on our mountain peak of faith and look back over "all the way the Lord has led us." We can recall having stood upon His promises and found ourselves on firm ground. And we have His continuing promises for today and tomorrow and always.

To think about and do:

Inflation can never touch my greatest assets.

Today is a good day for me to bring forth fruit.

A Reason for Tears

Psalm 126:5, 6; Revelation 7:17

I was visiting in a home where the mother wept as she told me about her unsaved son. The other children were happily following the Lord, while the much loved eldest, Michael, spurned the gospel. We were about to have lunch when the phone rang and my hostess excused herself. It was a lengthy call, and I can see her yet as she returned to the table. Her eyes were streaming, but she had a broad smile. She threw her arms around me and said, "It's *Michael!* He accepted the Lord last night. Oh, it's so wonderful I can hardly believe it—after all these years."

And all these tears, I thought. She had sown in tears; now she was reaping with joy. As we rejoiced together, I was reminded of what I had heard a wise minister say:

> When God sends tears it is so that
> He can follow them up with a rainbow.

Yet many people discount tears. We hear one say to another, "Don't cry—please don't cry." This is usually well intentioned; but it does nothing to help. Tear ducts are a part of our human equipment, and God gave them to us for a purpose.

Sometimes a child is more perceptive about tears than we who should know better. Cindy came home after playing with her little friend, Nancy, and she said to her mother, "Nancy's kitty died, Mama. Nancy was very sad, but I helped her," she assured her mother.

"How did you do that, dear?"

"I cried with her," Cindy explained.

John tells us our Lord himself wept. Those who stood around the tomb of Lazarus marked His tears and said, "Behold how he loved him!" (John 11:35, 36).

Some of the most inspiring words in all the Bible have to do with tears: "And God shall wipe away all tears from their eyes."

Who would not want to have some tears when *God* is going to wipe them all away?

To think about and do:

When I may not find the right words,
my tears can speak for me.

Tomorrow Unlimited

I'm *special* to God.
There is only one me.
I lift my head high at the prospect.
Not a piece or a pawn,
I'm a part of God's plan
And the blueprint He holds.
The design He'll reveal
One step at a time
As I yield to His will
My days and my hours—
My tomorrows unlimited.
I'm *special* to God.

Win the Argument—Lose a Friend

Proverbs 3:1-7

Angela couldn't keep a friend, and she could never figure out why. She liked people, was outgoing, and always willing to pull her weight when there was something to be done.

People, who at first welcomed her and included her in their doings would, after just a short time, shed her as they would shed a skin they could do without.

It was not unil another woman was concerned and caring enough to broach the subject that Angela began to wake up to what her problem really was. They talked a bit, then Angela interrupted saying, "Am I hearing you say that I always have to have the last word?" she asked in amazement.

"Not only that," the friend added, *"you always have to be right.* That alienates people."

You probably know people like Angela. They will argue and argue. Generally it's about something that doesn't matter and nobody can do anything about. I've heard such people do battle over whether it rained last Tuesday, or which day they had fish for dinner—and the word fight is on.

Now if there are two people, and one insists, "*I'm* right," what does this do for the other person? It's certainly no way to win or keep a friend. There's scarcely a surer way to fracture a relationship.

There has to be a great sense of insecurity in the "always-right" person who uses this tactic as an ego builder and then it backfires.

They are what the Bible calls wise in their own conceit; they lean to their own understanding, which is always a dangerous way to go.

Have you ever thought that Jesus could have said under any and all circumstances, "I am right"? And it would have been true. Our Lord would not stoop to such a practice, for it never fails to leave the one so put-down feeling angry and resentful. (There's a time to insist we're right: when truth and values are at stake. That's a whole other subject.)

Sadly, it's the phraseology that hurts. There's nothing remiss, for instance, in pointing out that something is in error, or is not accurate. It's the accusing 'You' that we react to—the "You are wrong" which is always inherent in "I am right."

We can be "right" every time—and go our lonely way—or we can acknowledge the trait and ask the Lord to help us overcome it.

To think about and do:

Only God is always right.

I'll settle for leaning on His understanding.

Three Hundred and Sixty-Six Fears?

Isaiah 41:10-14

The experts tell us that we come into this world with only two fears:

the fear of loud noises;
the fear of falling.

(Are you mentally counting all the things that cause *you* to fear?)

Many times I hear a person say, "I know the Bible keeps telling me to 'fear not'; but how *do* I, how can I *not* fear?" Then the person goes on to enumerate a whole array of fear-producing realities.

Everybody has fears. A few years ago a top scientist admitted, "*I'm* afraid, and all the aware men I know are afraid." Fear has become a sickness of our times. And with good reason. "Nobody is safe," we hear at least once a day.

For one of us to say to another, "Don't be afraid," would be a mockery. But *God* can say it.

And He does. Someone has compiled a list of the forms of "fear not" in the Bible. The total is 366—one for every day in the year and an extra for Leap Year!

Not all fears are to be gotten rid of. Some are useful warning signals. They alert us to take sensible action. Smoke warns of fire. Pain is a "friendly fear." It's the body's way of signaling, "See your doctor."

It's the fear that comes from daily living, from reading the newspapers with their graphic accounts of fearful happenings, from radio and television—fears that surround us and we can't do much, if anything, about them. It's for such fears the Lord has given us His promises.

The disciples showed fear when threatened by the storm-tossed Sea of Galilee. Why? Of all people, they should have been expected to remain calm? Were they not seasoned fishermen?

We need never have such a fear (nor should the disciples who knew the Lord Jesus so well). "Fear not, for I am with you; I am your God," is just one of the promises to hold on to in a "storm."

No one can live with moment-by-moment fear. A verse that has so many times come to my aid when I've been fearful is:

"What time I am afraid, I will trust in thee" (Psalm 56:3).

To think about and do:

I don't have to live in fear.

Today I will claim one of God's "fear nots" for myself.

What Singing Does for You

Isaiah 42:10-12; Ephesians 5:19

"Want to stay younger looking?" the announcement began. "Then join the church choir. Women who sing exercise their facial muscles—thus preventing wrinkles."

As I read it, I thought, *That's not a very noble reason for singing in the choir!* Anyway, what's so bad about a few wrinkles. Are we ashamed of the years the Lord has given us?

We do have a reason for singing. We sing because the Lord has put a song in our heart. We're not all prospects for the choir, but that need not keep us from singing to ourselves, from making melody in our heart unto the Lord. He isn't checking out the quality of our vocal performance.

From earliest record, music has been a part of human experience. Who taught music? Where did Jubal study organ and harp? (See Genesis 4:21.) The first *lyrics* come to us from Moses' song of victory, the song of redemption (Exodus 15). As New Testament believers, who has more to sing about than we do? And, apart from being an avenue of praise to God, singing has other benefits. It gives us an outlet to express our inner feelings. Singing also does something to our spirit. Can you, for example, remain angry with someone while you sing, "Jesus, Jesus, Jesus; There's just something about that name"? "Jesus, Jesus, Jesus—Sweetest name I know"? Can you really dwell on your loneliness while you're humming, "I never walk alone, Christ walks beside me"? Or any of your own favorite hymns?

We rob ourselves when we don't ever sing. We rob other people of joy and delight. A mother robs her children if they never hear her singing or humming a song as she goes about her work. I can never be thankful enough for a mother who sang. She sang beautiful hymns that stayed with me. When I became a Christian, I had this valuable store.

Some people, sadly, have no one to sing to. But that need not stop them. In fact it's a good reason for singing. Someone said to me a few days ago, "I live alone. I've nobody to talk to for days at a time. Some days I think I'm losing my voice from the lack of using it." And she added, with a shrug," I don't want to start talking to *myself.*"

"Why not try singing?" I suggested. "Sing along with a radio program or record. Or just *sing.*" Then I told her I do this all the time when I'm alone in my car. I praise the Lord and feel blessed and inspired.

A crowning reason for singing unto the Lord is that we are tuning up to join the heavenly choir.

To think about and do:

I may not be a soloist, but I can serve
the Lord with the voice He has given me.

Combating the Sameness

Lamentations 3:22-26

John, an eighty-year-old, is no whiner. But one day as I visited him in an attractive residence for seniors, he revealed his chief dissatisfaction with his way of life.

"It's the sameness, the awful sameness," he said ever so sadly.

Here is a man who all his life has been an inveterate reader and a daily walker; five miles a day was just a little jaunt for him. Now, his eyesight failing, he is robbed not only of the pleasure of reading but of the long leisurely walks he looked forward to each day. No more discoveries along the way; no more variety in his life. And the predictability of it all was getting to his spirit.

There's no pat Pollyanna solution to this problem. Age does bring a diminishing of one's faculties; we do have to adjust to less desirable circumstances. We can encourage each other, however, in the knowledge that God has new things for us each day if we will but look for them and expect them. Read verse 23 of our Scripture.

I know a Bengali man whose observation of God's handiwork led directly to his spiritual conversion. Daily, on his way to work, he crossed a field where wild flowers grew. As he took time to look at a certain plant, he became aware that each morning its leaves were tightly closed. As he retraced his steps in the early evening, the same plant had unfolded, and a flower looked up at him.

All his life this man had felt vague longings that his own religion did not satisfy. Pondering the phenomenon of the plant, one day—like a revelation from heaven—came the realization *there must be a God of the unfolding leaves!* He sought and found a Christian missionary who read God's Word to him and introduced him to the Son of the God of the unfolding leaves. Today, a committed believer, he writes and faithfully translates that others might be able to understand the God who meets the needs of his heart.

What if this man had just plodded through the field morning and evening, his eyes and mind closed to the wonders around him? He didn't.

It's not always possible for everybody to be close enough to observe God at work in plants and flowers, but God is always at work changing things, making them new and different. People are the most interesting subjects God works on. When we're willing to stop in our tracks to notice someone, who knows the exciting things it can lead to?

To think about and do:

God has an array of surprises to dispel the monotony.

Today I'm going to open my eyes and see.

Tomorrow Is for Faith

Father, You know if tomorrow holds
for me, grim tidings—
fruit of war.
You know if boasted faith
will stand this test—
if in quiet trust I'll rest
on Your unerring goodness, or
if hymns I've sung
of "anchor" and of "stay"
avail for only the sunny day.
Forbid it, God,
I should fail You so,
for tomorrow is for faith.
I know.

Someone to Rejoice In

Habakkuk 3:17-19

It's not always easy to rejoice. I have to confess I'm not like the person who wrote, "I feel like singing all the time."

Yet the Bible has much to say to us about rejoicing. Even so, we tend to excuse ourselves with such explanations as:

"If you knew my home situation, and what I have to endure."

"With my health problems, how *can* I rejoice?"

"What do *I* have to rejoice about—with a fixed income and inflation eating it up?"

Understandable. Nevertheless the word comes to us in every generation: "Rejoice evermore" (1 Thessalonians 5:16). *Evermore!* Paul strengthens this directive with "Rejoice in the Lord always" (Philippians 4:4), regardless of anything and everything. It is when we do rejoice in the face of trial and tragedy that God is glorified.

What if Paul and Silas had sat around in that Roman prison griping, maybe railing at God for what had happened to them? What if they had been sulking instead of singing? Would we have the Philippian jailor convert as an inspiring example of how to be saved? (I heard a preacher say, "If I had been Silas in that jail, Paul would have been singing a solo.") What then is the key to rejoicing evermore, under all circumstances? Rejoicing *in the Lord.*

Habakkuk sets a great example for us. Against all odds, natural disasters robbing him of his crops, his fruit, his meat, his milk, his oil, no hides and wool for clothing—almost everything that sustained his life taken away—he vowed,

> "Yet I will rejoice in the Lord, I will
> joy in the God of my salvation."

In this, Habakkuk evidenced his complete trust and confidence in God. Such a decision was a distinct act of the will: "I will rejoice."

We never do anything until we will to do it.

We might ask, "What benefit is there in rejoicing?" Plenty. Number one, it makes us feel better, because we're obeying what the Bible tells us to do. Secondly it gives credibility to our profession of Christ. People looking on can sense that we're "for real"; they know that in the same circumstances they would probably be doing everything but rejoicing.

There will never come a time when we cannot, *if we will to,* rejoice in the God of our salvation.

To think about and do:

If I grumble instead of rejoicing, how does my life differ from my unsaved neighbor's?

Getting Your Name in God's Book

Malachi 3:16-18

Few of us will ever see our name in a *Who's Who*. Nor are we likely to make the *Guinness Book of Records*—and that won't matter much. There are two books, however, that your name *can* be in. The choice is yours. The first book is *The Lamb's Book of Life*. Its pages are reserved for those who have accepted Jesus as Lord and Savior, who are "washed in the blood of the Lamb."

Entries in the second, *God's Book of Remembrance*, are likewise exclusive. These names record:

> They that feared (revered) the Lord;
> They that thought about His Name
> (only God can read our thoughts);
> They that spoke often one
> to another about the Lord.

What would keep us from thinking about the Lord and making Him the subject of our conversation one to another? Sometimes it's the lack of good models in our early Christian days. I thank God for the Christian man who, when I first knew the Lord, always quoted Malachi 3:16 rather than giving a testimony. I might have gone for years not ever knowing this powerful inspirational verse was in the Bible. As it was, because it spoke volumes to me, I learned it early.

Sometimes it's timidity that prevents us from talking about the Lord. Yet, just by channeling a dead-end conversation (about diets or inflation or "all the bad news") into *talking about the Lord,* can change all kinds of things. It can halt cruel gossip; it can put a rainbow where clouds have dominated as people have reinforced each other's gloom; it can pour oil on troubled conversation waters.

When we're talking about God, we have an ally in the Holy Spirit. He will take the things we say and make them real to people who need to hear.

Malachi tells us they spoke *often*—not just periodically in groups and scheduled classes, and as they milled around the temple after worship. "One to another"—neighbor with neighbor, friend with friend. How much we can influence other people as we spontaneously, out of our heart's love for God, talk about Him! I, for one, would not be sitting writing this material—and rejoicing as I do in the truth of it—if someone had not cared enough and *dared* enough to change the subject and talk about the Lord in my hearing.

To think about and do:

Thank God my name is in *The Lamb's Book of Life.*

I'm going to make sure it also gets into *God's Book of Remembrance.*

A Secret of Acceptable Giving

Matthew 6:1-4

To teach His disciples who were not all that quick to learn, the Lord Jesus painted word pictures for them. Here, the lesson is about the shortsightedness of showy giving.

Jesus portrays someone with a trumpeter preceding him as he goes into the temple to give an offering to God, or when he does an act of kindness to someone on the street. These were the religionists of that day, but they were no pattern for us to follow.

Was Jesus teaching that the secret of acceptable giving is giving in secret? I think so.

I remember a funeral service I attended where one after another came to the bereaved family members and said, "I'll always remember Bob." Then they would cite some instance when he had helped them in a time of need. "I don't know how I would have managed without him," one person summed it up.

That man surely had a reward to look forward

to. Meanwhile, his sons and daughter and grandchildren were blessed because of what they were hearing.

In restricting our giving to "not being seen by men," Christ hit at the favorite words in our vocabulary: "*I* gave," "It was given by *me*," "I've given *mine*," "*My* finances built that," "*I* paid for it *myself*,"—all in the context of the Lord's work.

Christ did us a favor by instructing us to give in secret. There is a peculiar satisfaction in doing something anonymously—in being responsible for carrying out a loving benevolent act without receiving praise or recognition. This is more than a "magnificent obsession" feeling; it's an inner glow that warms a person all over.

In addition, Jesus promised, when we do not seek the plaudits or thanks of one another down here, we are assured of a reward in Heaven. Since everything else in Heaven will be on the scale of "eye hath not seen, nor ear heard," we can afford to wait, confident that we will not be disappointed.

By contrast, "They have their reward," said Jesus of the trumpeted givers.

To think about and do:

Why eat my reward cake now?

Today I'll make sure of a reward in Heaven.

The Power of a Hymn

Matthew 11:28; John 14:1-3

Busy in my office, I was barely aware of the background music until I was arrested by the strains of, "Come home, come home."

Just then a secretary came along, and I said, "That's an old hymn, Pat." She listened. A faraway look came into her eyes, then she said, "Jeanette, that hymn—especially one line of it—was what first told me and made me feel that God loves me. It told me that He has a home and that He wants me to be there. He's calling me, the hymn told me. He's calling me tenderly."

Obviously the hymn had had life-changing meaning for her. For a moment she went back to the place and time the beautiful words had first spoken to her heart and met her needs. And she isn't pinning her hopes of a heavenly home on some lovely words set to music which happened to make her feel good on a long ago day. The Lord Jesus Christ *does* call. Jesus *is* tender. He *does* invite us to be with Him in that home He has gone to prepare. And the faithful Holy Spirit used a hymn to make all of this clear to my friend, Pat. Such is the power of a hymn.

Have you ever thought about how readily you

can recall the lines of a favorite hymn? Someone hums the tune and, without effort on your part, the words flow into your mind.

Time does not appreciably change this ability to remember hymns.

When visiting with a church group in a seniors' home, I've noticed some residents who waved off the offered hymnbook. "I can't see the print" is their understandable reason. Then I have seen these same men and women enter wholeheartedly into the singing. They knew the words by heart and reveled in singing them.

Sometimes when we need it most, a hymn will provide comfort, encouragement, or a sense of security. For me it might be the haunting, "I Will Pilot Thee," with its "Fear thou not, for I'll be with thee"; or that lovely Swedish hymn, "More secure is no one ever, than the loved ones of the Savior." Such hymns can change the climate of our day, give us confidence and strength to keep on going.

Let's thank God for the wealth of hymns that is ours, and for those whom He inspired to write them, as we call to mind our special favorites.

To think about and do:

Today I'll *listen* as God speaks to me
through an old familiar hymn.

The God for Every Hour

Tonight there came to me
The wondrous thought—
God slumbers not!

What if—
God had His hours
For meeting human need
And I might come too late—
Find God asleep.
What then?

Or if—
God worked in one time zone alone
And slept the hours between?
How could we safely rest
East—or West?
But God He slumbers not.

Why should I then
Not sleep
While God His watch does keep
O'er loved ones far away in distant zone.
I sleep—God sleepeth not.
Wondrous thought!

Making the Most of Your Quiet Time

Mark 1:32-35

Do you sometimes feel that the world is pressing in on you; that people are making demands on every minute of your time; that the whole town is at your door?

The Lord Jesus is our perfect example of how to cope with such frustrations and "impossibilities."

We will never be as busy as He was while He dwelt among men. But we have the same source of renewal. I've always been inspired by the words of the poem, "The Secret" that begins:

I met God in the morning
When the day was at its best.

In some religions, "meeting God in the morning" is mandatory. How often, in my work in Muslim countries, I've been awakened before dawn with the plaintive cry of the "muezzin," the Muslim Call to Prayer. And, wherever "the faithful" are or however sleepy they may be, they must obey this summons to prayer.

I would hesitate to insist that first thing in the morning is the only or even the best time for every Christian. When it is possible to spend time with God first thing in the morning, we rob ourselves when we let the other things take priority. Satan will work overtime to keep us thinking, *I'll find time during the day*. I know! He's been successful all too often in my own life.

There are all kinds of helps for your quiet time. They can be inspirational and motivating, but there's not much in most of these helps on the subject of being quiet; not much "be still." Paul knew the importance of a quiet time. He instructed the Christians of his day to *study to be quiet* (1 Thessalonians 4:11).

Some time ago, I heard George Beverly Shea sing, "Fill My Cup, Lord." It's a beautiful hymn, and it haunted me. I kept singing snatches of it over and over. Then I began to take in what I was asking the Lord to do in my life. It came to me that I probably don't keep quiet before the Lord long enough for Him to fill or even partially fill my cup.

There are times when we seek the Lord with a heart full of praise; at other times our approach to Him is a grocery list of needs and wants. And God, who knows all about us, graciously meets us where we are.

To think about and do:

If my quiet time must be one-way communication,
I want *God* to do the speaking.

God's Christmas Slogan

John 3:16; 1 John 4:14

Sometimes the advertising world can phrase for us what we mean better than we can ourselves. Such is the greeting-card logo, "When you care enough to send the very best."

God could have blazoned in the skies on that first Christmas night, "I cared enough to send Heaven's very best."

God *cared*. What else would motivate the Creator to plan such a gift for humanity yet unborn!

God cared *enough*. What is "enough"? We can never hope to plumb the depths or measure the heights of God's "enough" in the light of His *so great* gift. We *can* rest in the knowledge that it *is* enough to atone for our sins and fit us for our heavenly home, if we *accept* His gift.

God cared enough to *send*. We will never comprehend what it cost our heavenly Father; we *can* rejoice that the Father sent His Son to be the Savior of the world. From beyond the bounds of space, from the very throne of glory, God sent His Christmas gift.

No doubt about it. *God cared enough to send the very best.* We can say reverently, that God is a big spender. He could have sent an angel, but that would not have been enough. God's giving is the measure of His caring: God so loved that He gave His only Son.

And because God sent His gift of love, for nearly 2000 years the world into which Jesus came has celebrated Christmas. For a few days each year it is as though mankind were experiencing the wonder and the joy of that first Christmas. An inexplicable difference marks man's attitude toward his fellow man. A changed spirit prevails. The wonderful alchemy of Christmas causes the selfish to become less selfish, the unkind to exhibit some of the milk of human kindness, and the unloving to reach out with a degree of love.

Fortunately, we don't have to understand Christmas in order to benefit from the gift God sent to us. All we have to do is open our hearts, confess our sins, and accept and follow for ourselves God's Son from Heaven, the perfect gift that God cared enough to send.

To think about and do:

This Christmas, in addition to coming and adoring Him,

I will seek specific ways to share God's gift with others.

Chosen and Appointed

John 15:10-16

It's a wonderful feeling to be chosen. Can you remember when as a fifth or sixth grader you stood first on one foot then the other, impatient to hear your name called for a place on the class team? When you heard your name, you eagerly stepped over to the "chosen" circle. When you were left out, oh the disappointment

Some people never know the joy of being chosen to be a part of something. And they grow up feeling, "I don't *belong* anywhere; nobody seems to need me." I admit to having had some such feelings. As middle child in our family, I was never old enough for special favors; never young enough to escape doing the chores that kept me from reading a book (my favorite pursuit).

It was a memorable day for me, when, as a brand-new Christian, my eyes lighted on a verse that just seemed to pop up from the page:

"Ye have not chosen me,
but I have chosen you."

What a feeling! *Me*—chosen by God in Heaven! Later I read that God had made this choice away back before the foundation of the world (Ephesians 1:4). It was no last minute matter.

The Lord doesn't stop at *choosing* us. He has something for us to do subsequent to His choosing us.

"I have chosen you, and ordained you." (New American Standard Version says *"appointed* you.") We are not on a random walk that will ultimately take us to Heaven. No. We are on a God-appointed mission. The Lord has decreed that each one of us should produce something that shows we are His, that we are branches of the true vine.

We are to bring forth fruit. What kind of fruit? God will require of us only such fruit as springs from the seed He has implanted in us. We will, on that day when we stand before Him, have to give an account of what we have done with what He has entrusted to us.

Our fruit is to be the kind that *remains*—not necessarily some exotic kind such as heroic deeds and so on. It will be the daily acts of love and kindness and thoughtfulness that bless people; the cups of cold water in the name of the Lord.

In the midst of our often hectic schedules we will pause and ask, "What fruit am I producing today?" We can't excuse ourselves by saying, "Oh, I'm too old for that." The Bible says we "shall still bring forth fruit in old age." (See Psalm 92:14.)

To think about and do:

Jesus chose me.
Today I'm choosing to
produce some fruit for His name.

For Believers Only

John 17:20-26

The sermon had been on "The Chief End of Man." On his way out of church a young boy had said to the minister, "Sir, you told us what is the chief end of man. What is the chief end of *God?*"

Caught temporarily out of his depth, the minister complimented the boy for listening so well. Then he said, "Next Sunday we'll talk about what you asked."

"Oh, Sir, I don't have to wait till next Sunday. I *know* the answer. The chief end of God is to glorify man and enjoy him forever."

Out of the mouths of babes—

We're all familiar with the definition: The chief end of man is to glorify God and enjoy Him for ever. How wonderful to know that *God will be enjoying us* throughout eternity. As for glorifying us, the Lord Jesus prayed for this very thing (v. 22).

Lest we feel that this great prospect was for His disciples and other believers of that day only, we have the comforting assurance of verse 20:

> "Neither pray I for these alone, but for them also which shall believe on me through their word."

You and I are included *because we believe*.

Along that same line we have Revelation 4:11 which tells us that God created all things and that for His pleasure they are and were created. (Note the ongoing "are"; no stopping with one generation or another.)

Life may not hold much pleasure for some people. They may not be able to go outdoors and enjoy walking, feasting their eyes on God's ever-changing trees and flowers; they may not be able to hear the song of the birds or any of nature's glories. How blessed, then, to realize that the day is coming—for believers only—when Psalm 16:11 will be realized:

> "In thy presence is fulness of joy; at thy right hand there are pleasures for evermore."

We can confidently add, "That will be glory, be glory for me."

To think about and do:

If I have any doubts that *I really am a believer,* I will seek the Lord and pray for assurance.

The God of Tomorrow

With my limited sight narrow vistas I see;
God's eye encompasses the heavens—
And me.
He sees my today and He sees my tomor-
row—
What the hours will bring
Of joy and of sorrow.
No happening comes a surprise to my
God
And He has promised to share all my load.
He who marks even the sparrow's fall
Will surely hear me when I call.
Why should I worry?
Rather, I'll pray
To the God of tomorrow
Who leads the way.

The Last Red Letter Verse

Acts 1:1-8

Many Bibles have the words of Jesus printed in red. Reading in one such Bible a few days ago, I was struck by the significance of the last red verse on the page; even more so when it dawned on me that it was *the last sentence Jesus spoke* before ascending back to Heaven. It was His marching orders to the ones He was counting on to spread the gospel: "Ye shall be witnesses unto me" (v. 8).

Last words have special significance. Generally we will go to any extreme to carry out the wishes or commands of a dying loved one. Why, then, can we call ourselves believers, people who love Jesus Christ, and be so unheeding or dilatory about fulfilling His last directive? Jesus didn't say, You *may* be witnesses; you *shall*.

Can it be that we don't take the word "witness" at its face value? Instead, we wrap it in all kinds of trappings until it seems something that only very special persons can do.

What *is* a witness? It is someone who has firsthand knowledge of the thing in question. Nothing makes for more credibility than to be able to say, "I was *there;* I *saw;* I *know* what happened. (This is the only evidence permissible in a court of law.)

People can pooh-pooh our theories. They can dispute our reasoning or argument. They cannot refute our personal experience. I like the old hymn that goes,

"I was there when it happened,
and I ought to know."

Have you ever thought that you have a testimony for Christ that no one else in all the world has? I love to be in a group when one person starts to tell how he or she came to Christ. Others want to get in on this, and there are as many varied stories as there are people present.

The apostle Paul knew the inestimable value of personal testimony. He could have dazzled an audience with his knowledge and eloquence. He could have bragged about his family background every time he had the opportunity. But he chose not to, opting instead to tell of his life-changing encounter with the living Christ on the Damascus road.

No one else in recorded history had that same experience. But your coming to the Savior, and mine, is not less important—and our neighbors and friends need to hear it.

To think about and do:

I do have something to say for Christ.

I can—I will be His witness.

Formula for Change

Romans 12:1, 2; 2 Corinthians 3:18

Grandma Andrews had observed her small granddaughter, Angela, gaze long at a portrait in the upstairs hall. The child did this same thing every time she visited, and one day Grandma asked, "Why do you so much like looking at the lady in the picture, dear?"

"Oh, Grandma," the little seven-year-old replied, "the lady in the picture is *so bee-utiful!*" She sighed and said, "And, Grandma, I would like to be just like her."

Angela did not spell out, "Maybe—if I keep looking long enough—her beauty will rub off on me." She was too young for such reasoning. She likely had never even heard of "imaging" as a means toward change. But she was on the right track! For it is a fact that we do tend to become like that which we admire greatly.

The "looking" as a way to change cannot, however, be a casual glance once in a while. It has to be a consistent, regular pursuit. The clue is given in the phrase looking *as in a glass* (mirror)—with that degree of constancy. How often do we look in a mirror!

The Bible teaches that if we aspire to be like Jesus, we must major on looking at Him (through His Word) at least as frequently as we look in the mirror.

The change will take time; it will be gradual. But if we don't give up, we will by degrees begin to take on some of the lovely characteristics of the Lord we love. Something of His beauty and compassion will begin to be reflected in our attitudes and behavior toward those around us.

We may not notice the changes ourselves, but how gratifying when others do. The disciples did not know that their appearance (or behavior) gave them away. It was people looking on who saw them and took note "they had been with Jesus."

It's written of Moses, "He knew not that the skin of his face shone." But the people in the camp of Israel knew! Moses had spent time in the presence of God, and even the rebellious Israelites were awed by the change in their leader (Exodus 34:29).

Spending time with the Lord will cut out some of the time we allot to lesser things that will eventually leave their imprint upon us. Ultimately, then, the question comes down to this: Into whose image do I want to grow and change? That question settled, we can proceed toward being transformed into the image of Christ, which is God's intent for all His children, whatever our age.

To think about and do:

It's never too late to start changing.

Today I'll take a fresh look at my priorities.

But I Don't Have Any Gifts

Romans 12:6-9

Over their regular Sunday brunch, Grace and Mildred were discussing the sermon of the morning.

"What the pastor said about using our God-given talents was fine," said Mildred, "except what about people like me? I'm not all that sure that I have any. Also, isn't it a bit late for you and me to be thinking about that at our age?"

"Oh, come now," Grace smiled reassuringly. "Of course you have some gift. Doesn't everybody?"

The answer to Grace's question is yes.

Paul writes, "Having then gifts . . ." There is no room for doubts or questions. And the inference is that we should use these gifts.

The logical question then might be, "How do I know what my gift is?" I like Dr. Clyde Narramore's thinking along this line. He tells people,

> Your natural abilities are God's
> suggestions for your life's work.

So, how does a person find out, if he has not

already done so, where his natural abilities lie? I have found personally, and in working with other people, that the things we dream about doing is a vital clue to our God-given talents. True these dreams may appear to be impossibly out of reach for us during much of our life. However, many people, some of whom have dragged themselves year after year to a job they disliked, are in their later years activating their dreams, turning them into goals, and finding both success and fulfillment.

Not all of God's gifts are for doing; some are for just being. I once heard a woman (like Mildred) say, "I have no gifts or talents." The words were hardly out of her mouth when a young woman spoke up, "Oh, yes, you have! You're good at sitting by the fire and being a friend." The world will never have enough such friends. Increasingly people are dying for lack of someone to sit down and just be there. And think! To do this, you don't have to go back to college and take courses. You don't have to buy equipment. You don't have to be clever or have all the answers. You do have to be a tolerably good listener (which is probably what the quick-to-speak-up young woman meant by "being a friend").

Never discount *any* gift God has given you. No one else can ever exercise it quite the way you can, and the world will be the poorer if you do not use it.

To think about and do:

The ability, the talent, is God's gift to me. Making use of it is my gift to God.

More Than a Wall Motto

Romans 12:16-21

"Blessed are the peacemakers."

So reads the motto in some homes. It's a great attitude to aim for we'll no doubt all agree. But the role of a peacemaker doesn't come naturally to most of us.

Was Paul, in his "as much as lieth in you, live peaceably," giving us an out for the times we find it difficult to get along with someone? A verse to salve our conscience?

On the surface this might appear to be so. But let's look a little deeper. What lies inside us as Christians? Does not the Holy Spirit. And cannot He empower us to cope with unpleasant situations and still maintain our Christian witness?

Human nature being what it is, some people are going to rub us the wrong way (as we ourselves do to other people). And it does take a brand and a degree of grace that we don't always seem to have when we need it.

Perhaps if we took into consideration that something caused the other person to be and to act as he does—something in his background and experience that would probably have made *us* just as hard to get along with—we might be more tolerant and understanding. Or we might take another look at ourselves.

A friend shared with me this experience which taught her a lesson:

"I dreaded my sister-in-law's visits. Besides preparing for her, I tried to prepare myself. I prayed extra hard that things would go well. And for an hour or so everything would be fine, at least on the surface. Then something she said or did would get to me and I would tense up and—Oh, it was *unbearable,*" she confided. "Then, one day I ran upstairs and snatched time to pray for grace. Right then it came to me, *Could she be having to spend extra time praying for grace to put up with me!* I searched my own heart, asked the Lord to forgive me for thinking only of my own feelings and always expecting the worst of my sister-in-law, and to give me some real love for her. I don't know how much this changed her; I do know it changed me. I *could* live peaceably with her. We never became close and loving. But neither was our relationship an armed truce. Her visits became almost a pleasure to look forward to."

Ultimately, Christ himself is the real peacemaker, "having made peace through the blood of his cross" (Colossians 1:20).

If we will let Him, He will give each of us a ministry of peacemaking, and He will supply the needed grace to practice peacemaking. The reward? We will be called *the children of God.*

To think about and do:

A motto on a wall can't speak as effectively as a life that demonstrates it.

Tomorrow Is for Beginning Again

Tomorrow—
The day of beginning again—
The day when a wish can come true.
If I had one more chance
To start over again
I know how much better I'd do.

I would love and forgive
And strive to live
Better than ever before—
With more thought for others
And less for myself
In that day of beginning once more.

So I thank You, God,
For a day that's all new
A day of beginning again—
And I pray I'll be worthy
To stand before You
At the close of the day—Amen.

Nobody's Getting Any Younger

1 Corinthians 13:1-13

Five-year-old Jenny asked her mother, "Why are old people so grouchy?" (To Jenny almost everybody was "old.")

The mother answered as best she could. The fact is that no group, young, old, or inbetween can be catagorized as one thing or another. We are individuals.

Nevertheless, little Jenny's question is worth thinking about whatever our age. For what we will be later, we are presently becoming.

There's much study, speculation, experimentation—and even more talk—on the matter of "Aging." But we can't escape the fact that no one is getting a day younger. Many of us can reasonably anticipate longer years of retirement and so forth. But each added day will be another challenge to get along with those around us.

If you *want* to become crotchety—maybe even obnoxious—here's a way to start:

Never listen to anyone else.
Expect the worst of everybody.
Demand your "rights."
Respect nobody's opinion but your own.
Keep your feelings out where they can easily get hurt.
Remember every little injury anyone ever did you.

There are others, but these are a beginning.

The Bible offers a total course in "How to Grow Old Gracefully." The short course is complete in "The Love Chapter." Let's look at verses 4-7:

Loves' Dos and Don't

> Love is very patient and kind, never jealous or envious, never boastful or proud, never haughty or selfish or rude. Love does not demand its own way. It is not irritable or touchy. It does not hold grudges and hardly even notices when others do it wrong. It is never glad about injustice, but rejoices whenever truth wins out. If you love someone you will be loyal to him no matter what the cost. You will always believe in him, always expect the best of him, and always stand your ground in defending him.

The encouraging thing about God's "How Tos" is that He enables us by the power of the indwelling Holy Spirit to *work* on them. Not all at once, but little by little we can put this chapter into practice. In the doing of it, we'll make life easier for ourselves and for other people.

To think about and do:

I'm not getting any younger, either.

So—I'm going to consider taking up this challenge.

Good—and Good for You

Ephesians 4:1-7

Paul, from his Roman prison, is apparently concerned about the unity among the believers in Ephesus.

David in his day wrote,

> "How good and how pleasant it is
> for brethren to dwell together
> in unity" (Psalm 133:1).

Good and pleasant: a hard to find combination most of the time.

Can you recall during your childhood—and later—someone urging you to, "Take this; it's good for you"? You were then handed a foul-tasting concoction. Dutifully you gulped it down, mentally resisting and wondering why something that's good for you has to taste so bad.

The psalmist and Paul knew the value and the necessity of unity. It's good for everyone concerned when we pull together in a common purpose. It also makes for pleasant working conditions.

As Christians we have this mandate to

endeavor—for it's not always easy—to keep the peace among ourselves in the bonds of unity.

Some Christians manage to fit the pattern, to be the perpetual unity makers, but they're not all that pleasant. As often has been said, "Saints are hard to live with."

It's so refreshing to find a fellow Christian who is both good and good to be with.

There's a never ruffle anybody's feathers; never rock the boat kind of unity. Without solid convictions, its aim is peace and unity at any price. This is not what either Paul or David had in mind.

It's an interesting simile that David used when he likened the good and pleasant relationship of the brethren to "perfume," the oil used on and by the priests. It was no Chanel # 5 type concoction. It was a special formula given by the Lord himself. (See Exodus 30:34-36.)

Does that ointment savor of the fragrance of Christ? Is that the secret formula for so living for Him that we *can* be both good and pleasant?

This unique fragrance is not for everybody. As in Old Testament days, it is reserved for priests, and God has made us priests. So we can spread the fragrance about. This will make us both good and good for others around us.

To think about and do:

I'm going to search my heart and ask the Lord to make me a good and pleasant witness for Him.

In the School of Suffering

Philippians 1:19-30

How many people would voluntarily enroll in the school of suffering if it were to advertize "enrollment open"? I'm sure I wouldn't.

Yet the Bible calls suffering a gift: "Unto you it is given," Paul tells us, "not only to believe on him, but also to suffer."

Enrolled in this school, we can be sure we have the Master Teacher. God is also the Master Designer. He knows how best to perfect that which He has created. God is not toying with ceramics; He is molding us for eternity. It's not always a pleasant experience. Often, we would prefer not to learn, not to be reshaped.

But—and it will take a thousand eternities to explain or understand this—God's divine alchemy produces peace out of pain, sweetness out of sorrow, and beauty from ashes. Who can dispute this? The serenity on the face of the chronic sufferer, the peace-filled expression when pain furrows the brow, the sweet contentment of a poor, deprived elderly saint when the very opposite would be more understandable. In my early days as a Christian, one of the greatest inspirations to me and to fellow new converts was a woman we called Mother Young. She had little of what the world would say makes for contentment, but her favorite hymn, which she taught all of us just by singing it so often, was:

> "I have Christ;
> What want I more?"

The radiance in her face was something to behold. When some of us get together, we still talk of Mother Young and her influence upon us.

Suffering comes in many forms—none of them easy to accept. Yet, as Amy Carmichael has so eloquently expressed it, "In acceptance lieth peace."

Unquestionably, the most difficult thing to accept is death, our own or that of someone we deeply love. We know intelligently that "it is appointed unto men once to die." We recite, "to die is gain," and "absent from the body" means being "present with the Lord." As Christians we would strongly defend our position on this truth. But we have our emotions to deal with; and our emotions make us shrink from meeting this "last enemy."

It's a well-established belief that normally there are three reactions to oncoming death: *denial:* "Everybody dies—but not me; not now"; *blame:* "Why didn't I get better treatment? etc."; thirdly, *acceptance.*

The true believer, as he gives up fighting it, has the assurance that God has not forsaken him.

To think about and do:

I can be patient in God's school of suffering, for one day I will graduate into His presence.

"How To" Is Not Enough

James 1:22-27

We step up to an information desk and ask for directions on how to get to a certain place. Then we act on that information.

But there's another whole area of information-seeking these days. "We're running from seminar to seminar and filling our heads with a variety of new knowledge. And, of course, it's good to keep one's mind open and our horizons broadening. There's nothing wrong with the pursuit of knowledge. It's what we do with what we know to do that matters.

Just having a whole new area of information and doing nothing about it would be tantamount to buying a new cookbook and never trying even one recipe. That book, no matter how interesting its cover, left on your kitchen shelf or counter is useless: it will never produce a luscious pie or a batch of hot rolls. You might just as well have admired it, and then left it in the store.

What if the seminar we attend focuses on *Bible memorization?* We get all inspired and begin to do something about it. In a few weeks of diligent application, we've mastered quite a few key verses. (Let me digress to pass on from my friend, Dr. Ralph Byron, himself a walking Bible, this fact which he passed on to his Sunday-school class: "We can all memorize; it just takes us a little longer as we get older. That means that what a younger person takes twenty minutes to memorize will be about 23 for the rest of us.")

So what is lacking, once we have the knowledge?

Probably it's motivation. We're not sufficiently moved by the needs of the people around us who may never have been effectively told that God loves them and that Jesus died for them. Yet, they are there: the fear-filled men and women; the insecure; the lonely and unloved; and—let's face it—the *lost* ones, until they have accepted Christ as their Savior.

Not only can we be a blessing as we share what we're learning, but James tells us that we will be blessed for our deed.

Have you considered that one of the best ways to fasten a thing in our own minds is to practice it. Otherwise we can become what the practical James calls "a forgetful hearer."

To think about and do:

There's a time to learn,
and a time to be a doer.

Tomorrow Is For . . .

Who's better that I've lived today,
I wonder?
Do some whose lives I've touched today—
as memory plucks me from the score of hours and
  four,
warm, and a smile play on their faces,
a smile that's there
because my life touched theirs today?
        And if not, God—
if no brief rush of warmth exists
to say
        I've cheered one person on his way,
today,
        That's what tomorrow's for!

What—Fear Tomorrow!

Tomorrow's at my door, God.
I shrink. I take a halting, backward step
For what I do not know I dread
As fog on a winding, hilly road
Curtaining the way ahead.
I fear tomorrow at my door.

But no!
Why should my heart—serene today
Because You are my Guide and Stay—
Not trust?
Tomorrow ticking at my door,
When strikes your hour
I'll meet you—not alone—
My God already there.

How can I know?
Today was yesterday's tomorrow.
And to quench all fear, I hear
A Voice that says,
"Behold! I am with you
All the days."